Earning Money from Internet Through Advertisement Websites

By

Dr. Hidaia Mahmood Alassouli

1) Introduction:

This book explains some easy ways for earning money from internet form advertisement websites. The book covers the following ways to earn money from internet and to increase the number of visitors in your website.

1. Introduction

2. Earning money through shortening the url of your website in the advertisement sites such as Adf.ly and Adfoc.us

3. Getting traffic to your website using Bot traffic tool.

4. Using "iView Fur U v3!" tool to bring traffic to your website.

5. Using "TBN Best Tuber" tool to bring traffic to your website.

6. Using "Adf.ly Bot 3.1.0" tool to bring traffic to your website.

7. Using "traffic sprite" tool to bring traffic to your website

8. Using "Hit leap" tool to bring traffic to your website

9. Using "otohits.net" tool to bring traffic to your website.

10. Online Ad Models: CPM, CPC, CPL, CPA

11. Top 15 Advertisement Network s

12. Best 6 Advertisement Networks

13. Creating blog website for advertisements in blogger.com:

14. Creating word press website for advertisements in www.wordpress.com

15. Creating word press website for advertisements in free webhosting www.000webhost.com:

16. Creating advertisement links in Propeller Ads and using them in the blogger website:

17. Creating advertisement links in Propeller Ads and using them in the word press website.

18. Creating advertisement links in revenue hits and using them in the word press website.

19. Earning money from advertisement links in CPAlead and using them in the word press website:

2) Earning money through shortening the url of your website in the advertisement sites such as Adf.ly and Adfoc.us

Earning money through shortening the url of your website in the advertisement sites such as Adf.ly and Adf.us

1. Register in adf.ly website. Put on it PayPal information to receive your payment. You will get the following image.

2. Shrink the link that you want to use it to earn money from it. For example, www.google.com
    is shortened to http://fasttory.com/Fe8H

3. You can use other website also Adfoc.us. Enter the PayPal email for payment. You will get
    this view.

4. I noticed the profit in Adfoc.us is less than adf.ly site

AdFoc.us
shrink share earn

⚠ You have incomplete account information.
Please update your account settings in order to be paid.

[▾ Follow @adfocusheb] [5,237 followers]   G+

Today's Earnings: $0.0000   **This Month's Earnings:** $0.0000   **Total Earnings:** $0.0000
Today's Clicks: 0   **This Month's Clicks:** 0   **Total Clicks:** 0

⦿ Single Link   ○ Multiple Links

http://   **SHRINK!**

AdFoc.us Announcements and Updates

Feb 07, 2018 | Payments for Jan 2018 have begun!

⁌ 25, | Payments for Dec 2017 completed.

5. Shorten a link on it. For example, www.amazon.com. I got the following link: http://adfoc.us/4623871

My Links

Show 10 ▾ entries   ☐ Show deleted   Search:

Link	Views	Earnings	Date Added ▾			
http://adfoc.us/4623871 *http://www.amazon.com*	0	$0.0000	Mar 24, 2018	✎	✖	☐

Showing 1 to 1 of 1 entries

First   Previous   **1**   Next   Last

Deleted Links	0	$0.0000
MY LINK TOTALS	0	$0.0000

3) Getting traffic to your website using Bot traffic tool.

There are many ways to get traffic to your website.

1- First you need to get the proxy list. You can use many utilities existing in the net. Some of these programs: Net Ghost, Proxy finder, Gather Proxy.

- If using Net-Ghost, download Net_Ghost_Latest.rar. Run the program while the antivirus is stopped. In the Grbber tab, grap proxies. In the checker tab, check the live proxies. Copy the checked proxies saved in the file in the folder or proxy downloader. Or you can get proxies form websites

- If using Gather Proxy. Download also the software. Then run Gather Proxy.exe. Then in the tab Gather Proxy, gather the proxies. In the tab Proxy checker, check the live proxies. Export the live proxies in txt file. Here the picture.

2- The shrink link of my website www.amazon.com in adfoc.us is http://adfoc.us/4623871. I want to bring visitors to this site.

3- You can find a lot of traffic bot tools in the net. I downloaded "Diabolic Traffic Bot v6.11 Full Edition Cracked +Proxy Tools.tar". Run the program TrafficBot Full Edition.exe . Here the output.

4- Go to edit and choose private proxies and paste the copied proxies from the file that you saved proxy list. Test for the live proxies and save them.

5- Choose the module to run adf.ly. It means "click next in adf.ly url."

6- Choose types of proxies to be private proxies.

7- Put in the module data section, in the url list tab, the url you wish to make traffic for it. For example, I put http://adfoc.us/4623871 many times.

8- . Put in the module data section, in the referrer tab, the referrer sites. You can copy around 500 sites from the file Top 500 Referrer Links.txt came with the program.

9- Click the start icon.

9

10- Note: I saw some increase in adf.ly for the number of views after using the program. So this method is effective for adf.ly and adfoc.us

6. There are some tools that can be used also. To bring traffic to your website. Some of them grouped in the compressed folder "BOT PARA ADFLY 2017".

4) Using "iView Fur U v3!" tool to bring traffic to your website:

1- One of the tools called "iView Fur U v3!". It definitely can bring traffic to your website. It can be found as one of the tools in "BOT PARA ADFLY 2017" compressed folder.

2- Open the tool Browse to the proxy file to load proxy list. Then type the url of your website. For example, http://www.youtube.com with short link http://fasttory.com/DVct in adf.ly

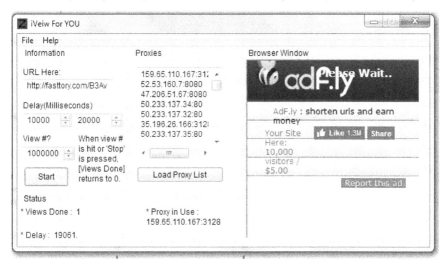

3- Note: I did not see any increase in adf.ly for the number of views after using the program. So this method is not effective for adf.ly and adfoc.us

5) Using "TBN Best Tuber" tool to bring traffic to your website:

11- One of the tools called "TBN Best Tuber". It definitely can bring traffic to your website. It can be found as one of the tools in "BOT PARA ADFLY 2017" compressed folder.

12- Open the tool Browse to the proxy file to load proxy list. Then type the url of your website. For example, http://www.yahoo.com with short link http://fasttory.com/ DaK2 in adf.ly

13- Note: I did not see any increase in adf.ly for the number of views after using the program. So this method is not effective for adf.ly and adfoc.us

6) Using "traffic sprite" tool to bring traffic to your website:

1- One of the tools called "traffic sprite". Download and open the tool. You will need to register then login. Then type the url of your website such as the shorten adf.ly link for http://www.skype.com is http://fasttory.com/ DgrZ. You can change the setting to those that can suite your website.

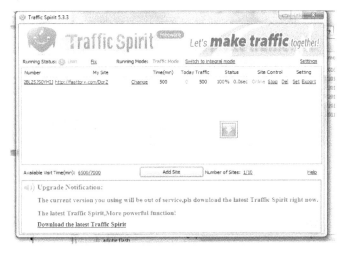

2- Note: I saw very few increases in adf.ly for the number of views after using the program. So this method may be effective for adf.ly and adfoc.us.

7) Using "Hit leap" tool to bring traffic to your website:

1- One of the websites that can give traffic in your behalf called hit leap. Open the website *https://hitleap.com*. You need to register then login. Then go to my web site and add the url of your website. Such as the shorten adf.ly link for http://www.google.com is http://fasttory.com/Fe8H

2- To earn traffic, download and install hit leap viewer from the link of earn traffic page to earn points that can be used to hit your website.

3- Note: I saw very little increase in adf.ly for the number of views after using the program. So this method may be effective for adf.ly and adfoc.us.

8) Using "otohits.net" tool to bring traffic to your website:

1- One of the websites that can give traffic in your behalf called otohits. Open the website *https:// otohits.net*. You need to register then login. Then go to my web site and add the url of your website. Such as the shorten adf.ly link for http://www.microsoft.com is http://fasttory.com/FiX9. Go then advanced options. Make it application only. Make timer 36 to 36. Go to clicks, and choose to click 2 to 2. Make activation to be 100% to 100%. We choose minimum waiting time 10 sec. So the advertisement will be for 36 sec. Install otohits.net viewer to earn traffic. See useful video https://www.youtube.com/watch?v=ySNcHMAalBY

2- To earn traffic, download and install otohitsApp from the link of earn traffic page to earn points that can be used to hit your website.

9) Online Ad Models: CPM, CPC, CPL, CPA

1. Cost per Thousand (CPM)

This is also known as "cost per mille." As a publisher, you charge a flat rate for one thousand displays, or impressions, of an advertisement to your audience. About 33% of internet ad revenues in 2013 were priced using CPM (up from 32% the previous year.) If your publication offers a highly-engaged audience with high-volume traffic and if your advertisers are more interested in brand exposure than making the immediate sale, CPM may be right for your publication.

2. Cost per Click (CPC)

CPC is one of several performance-based online ad models. Someone on your website clicks an advertisement, and you, as the publisher, are compensated for that action. Ad sales software can help control for accidental clicks and abuse. If you are trying to attract advertisers that want an immediate response, such as an online retailer, CPC may be the way to go. Well-designed layouts and advertising programs can limit the risk in moving from CPM to CPC.

3. Cost per Lead (CPL)

You can think of CPM, CPC, and CPL / CPA as a range, increasing the requirements for what a publisher must deliver to earn revenue. With **cost per lead**, advertisers compensate you when someone views an ad on your site, clicks that ad, and then takes a further action to become a qualified lead for a sale. This might mean signing up for an e-newsletter, reward programs, or free website membership. If your publication has a niche audience, your world of potential advertisers may be limited. A cost per lead or cost per acquisition relationship could mean that you work with fewer advertisers at a more involved level for higher compensation.

4. Cost per Acquisition (CPA)

Cost per acquisition is similar but has an even higher bar. Publishers only receive payment for completed sales (i.e. the e-newsletter subscriber goes on to purchase services from the advertiser.) If your publication has a niche audience, your world of potential advertisers may be limited. A cost per lead or cost per acquisition relationship could mean that you work with fewer advertisers at a more involved level for higher compensation.

10) Top 15 Advertisement Network s

1. Google AdSense

Google AdSense is recognized as the world's largest and best online advertising network. Most importantly, it's free and provides you the opportunity to earn money by placing ads on your website.
However, to get approved by Google AdSense is not easy. You have to follow AdSense quality guideline to get approved.

It is particularly known for serving CPC Ads and CPM Ads. It shows mobile ads, video ads, search result ads, display ads, and banner ads. The ads are relevant to your content. You can choose the type of ads that best fit your website. It has the largest network of online advertisers. It makes sure that only the highest paying ads go live on your website, so you get the most for your ads.

2. Propeller Ads

Propeller Ads is one of the fastest growing CPM Ads Network. It provides multiple Ad Formats. Propeller Ads makes it easy for you to select best-performing ad campaign. It serves various Ad Models such as CPM, CPC, CPA, and CPL. It ensures high ad quality by performing manual checks on advertisers. It provides publishers on-time payouts, detailed real-time reporting, and a personal account manager. It endeavors to provide the highest revenue per visitor. It has a multitude of display advertising solutions.

3. Revcontent

Revcontent is recognized as one of the most selective and premium native ad networks in the world. It has grown to be one of the biggest content recommendation platforms on the internet. It currently serves 100 billion content recommendations a month across the globe. However, Revcontent is highly selective in choosing publishers. It supports transparent reporting and easy customization options for publishers.

4. Infolinks

Infolinks is one of the best Ad Networks that enables publishers to monetize their website to the optimum level. It mainly provides In-Text CPM Ads. So, if you have a text based site or a blog, and then Infolinks might prove to be a great option for generating revenue by advertising on your website.

They don't cover spaces so you can use other banner ads from other Ad Network for earning revenue for site content. Infolinks Ads are targeted for any relevant keyword from your content. They have no minimum traffic requirement for publishers. Infolinks works with the biggest advertisers in the world such as Facebook, Amazon, eBay, Microsoft, etc.

5. Adsterra Network

Adsterra is another immensely popular premium ad network which serves as much as 50 billion geo-targeted ad impression a month. It provides Ad Models such as CPC, CPM, and CPA. It provides innovative advertising solutions for web and mobile advertisers and publishers worldwide.

Adsterra supports publishers from all verticals and assures monetization of their ad inventory. It provides various ad formats for the web and mobile platform including display banners, interstitial, popunders, direct links, sliders, and Pushup. It guarantees highest possible ad quality and security. Publishers get on-time payments.

6. Media.net

Media.net is one of the most popular Ad Network for Publishers. It provides a great opportunity to publishers to maximize revenue from their online content. It has one of the largest pools of advertisers in the world. Media.net serves contextual ads. It also supports desktop interstitial, in-content native, and mobile docked ads. It ensures a 100% fill rate across all verticals and ad formats. Some of its publishers include Reuters, Esquire, Elle, Forbes, Cosmopolitan, etc.

7. Revenue Hits

Revenue Hits is a PPC and CPM Ad Network for Publishers. It uses contextual and geo-targeted ad serving technology to serve ads on websites, mobile sites, add-ons, toolbar, widgets, and more. It serves over 1 billion ad impressions each day and provides 100% fill rate across all geographic locations. Besides display ads, Revenue Hits also enables publishers to monetize their site using pop-ups, text ads, apps, widgets, and other custom formats.

8. Bidvertiser

Bidvertiser Ad Network for Publishers provides interesting monetization model. Apart from providing PPC Ad Model wherein, a publisher earns money when an ad is clicked; the publisher also earns additional revenue when the click leads to a conversion (sale). Bidvertiser supports many ad formats such as banners, rectangles, skyscrapers, mobile, etc. Its reporting interface makes monitoring ad performance easy. You come to know click-through-rate, the amount you have earned as well as other information.

9. Clicksor

Clicksor is a Canada-based Ad Network. It serves over 900 million ad impressions on its publisher network sites. It offers various ad formats including banner ads, in-text ads, interstitials, rich media, layer ads, pop-up ads, pop-under, etc. It is a bid based CPC and CPM Ads Network.

Other Details:

Publisher Traffic Requirement: None

Minimum Payout: $50

Payment Method: e-check, bank transfer, PayPal

10. PopAds

PopAds is mainly a pop-under ad network. It is a fast, efficient and secure advertising network. Publishers can monetize their website traffic through high-quality pop-under ads. It offers competent rates to publishers which depend on website traffic and website content. It also offers perfect support as well.

11. AdCash

AdCash is a leading advertising network providing high-quality ads from leading brands at effective pricing models which are designed to increase revenue from your website. It supports Ad Models such as CPC, CPM, and CPA. It has a big ad inventory. Display formats include slide-in, background, interstitial, site under, footer, and more. There is no minimum traffic requirement for publishers.

12. Max Bounty

Max Bounty is a leading performance marketing network. It connects trusted and skilled affiliate marketers with high paying advertisers on a CPA basis. It is one of the biggest affiliate networks that you can trust to earn more, whether as an affiliate or as an advertiser. It works with the best advertisers and affiliates in the industry thereby cutting out fraud and mitigating risk.

13. ShareASale

ShareASale is a popular Cost per Sale Affiliate Network. It has an ethical and transparent business model, efficient technology, and reliable network platform. It has been operating successfully for more than ten years. It runs an Advanced Affiliate Marketing Platform with a strong network of advertisers and affiliates.

14. Chitika

Chitika is one of the largest Ad Network with over 300,000 publishers. It serves Ads on CPC Model. Its approval process for new publishers is pretty easy. Moreover, it does not have any minimum traffic requirement. With Chitika, you can make money if you have traffic. It provides you the right mix of ads with Real Time Bidding. It furnishes an online publisher control panel with which you can easily monitor your ad impressions and revenue. Chitika is constantly evolving and makes every effort to maximize your yield.

15. BuySellAds

BuySellAds is another rewarding Ad Network that connects publishers and advertisers. It allows publishers to set price for the Ad space on their website or blog. Advertisers can directly access the publishers on BuySellAds. The Ads are usually served on CPM Model. It functions as a marketplace for publishers and advertisers to buy and sell ads. However, its approval process is quite hard. The minimum traffic requirement is 15k visitors per month. The minimum payout is $20, and payment method is PayPal.

11) Best 6 Advertisement Network s

In the world of blogging, there is common problem from small bloggers to reputed bloggers either they don't get approval of new Blogs and websites or their AdSense account is banned for not good reasons. in this case some publishers think it is better to give up instead of funding lavish blog while others looking for new ad networks. at last their search ends up with many ad networks. but they are not familiar with such networks and they have not enough time to test theme one by one because lack of funds and other reasons. for the solution of such situations, these articles tell you about already tested best ads networks that instantly approved new Blogs and websites.

1. Popads

popads is the best Popad network for small publisher. PopAds.net offers high eCPM rates and 100% fill rates for publisher. It allows almost all sites. It provides publishers to daily withdrawal option which is unique from other ad networks. popads is best option for new Blogs and websites, there is no minimum traffic required for approval of new Blogs and websites. so, publishers can register with new blog and website and get approved within 24 to 48 hours.

2. Revenue hits

Revenue hits is the totally different from other ads networks and best platform for monetizing Blogs and websites, also best alternative of Google AdSense. Revenue hits offers high eCPM rates and Various ads models for monetizing websites. Revenue hits is CPA based ad network i.e. they pay you for clicks that goes to an action but don't pay for impression. For approval of new websites they apply very simple conditions. almost all sites are accepted except gambling, porn site and other adult related sites are not accepted. so, if you want to monetize your blog then sign up on Revenue hits as publisher and submit your website to Revenue hits. If your website has low traffic then doesn't worry because there no minimum traffic required.

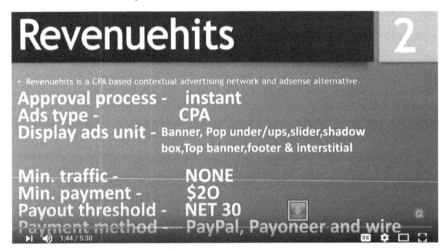

3. Adhitz

Adhitz ad network is based on CPC (cost per click) and approval of new Blogs and websites is very fast. Interesting things about adhitz is it offers fixed CPC rates for both publisher and advertiser .There are no minimum traffic required for new website. New publishers' sign up on Adhitz submit their site and get site approved immediately. They not accept gambling and porn site.

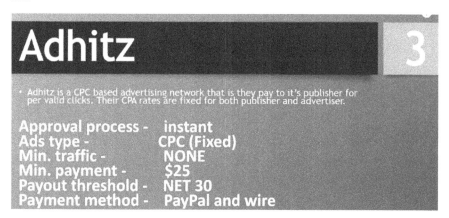

Adhitz 3

- Adhitz is a CPC based advertising network that is they pay to it's publisher for per valid clicks. Their CPA rates are fixed for both publisher and advertiser.

Approval process - instant
Ads type - CPC (Fixed)
Min. traffic - NONE
Min. payment - $25
Payout threshold - NET 30
Payment method - PayPal and wire

4. Clicksor

Clicksor is also best ad network for small publisher. It offers various ad formats like Google AdSense. Approval process of new site is very simple for this ad network. So for new bloggers, it is the best option to monetize their blog with Clicksor because there is no minimum traffic needs and weekly payout.

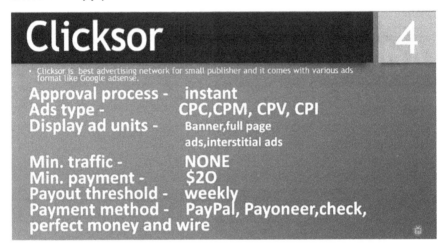

5. Infolinks

Infolinks offers highly advanced advertising tools publisher and most popularly known for their In tag ads because they are master in providing in tag ads . it is also alternative of Google AdSense. Infolinks does not affect AdSense, publishers can use both AdSense and infolinks together.

infolinks is game changing for that publisher whose most traffic comes from English speaking countries like US, Canada or UK. publisher agreement of infolinks is not too much strict as Google AdSense. hence there is no barrier for new bloggers, they simply register themselves as publisher on Infolinks official sign up page and submit their site. Approval of new site can take 48 to 72 hours. once your site is approved, your door of earning is opened.

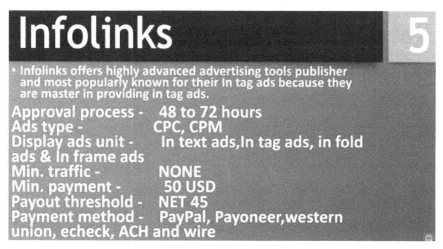

Infolinks

5

- Infolinks offers highly advanced advertising tools publisher and most popularly known for their In tag ads because they are master in providing in tag ads.

Approval process - 48 to 72 hours
Ads type - CPC, CPM
Display ads unit - In text ads,In tag ads, in fold ads & In frame ads
Min. traffic - NONE
Min. payment - 50 USD
Payout threshold - NET 45
Payment method - PayPal, Payoneer,western union, echeck, ACH and wire

6. Chitika

Chitika is a primary non contextual and display advertising network, which makes it different among all other advertising networks. They shows most relevant ads to visitors on the basis of search engine queries but not on the basis of keywords found on respective webpage that contextual ads networks shows like Google AdSense, hence to make more profit you can use together with AdSense because their ads showing method is different and do not affect one another. Chitika works best for those publishers whose most of traffics comes from search engines but not best for those publishers whose most of traffic comes from social networks. Interesting things about chitika is it offers low minimum payout via PayPal.

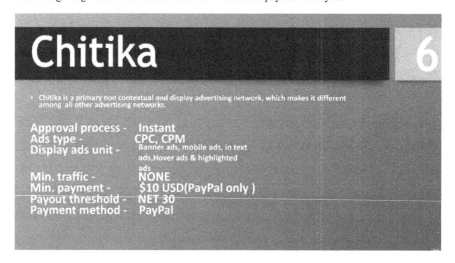

12) Creating blog website for advertisements in blogger.com:

1- See the video https://www.youtube.com/watch?v=obiWL93NYog for explanation.

2- Make a blog for your advertisement website. Go to https://www.blogger.com. Create your blog. You will get the following screen. I wrote title of my blog: Dr. Hidaia Alassouli Advertisement Blog. The web address of my blog halassouli-ad.blogspot.com. Choose the theme. I chose "Awesome Inc." theme

13) Creating word press website for advertisements in www.wordpress.com:

1- I created an account in https://wordpress.com/start/about?ref=create-lp. I put the title: "Dr. Hidaia Alassouli Advertisement" I named it:". halassouliadv.wordpress com". I put the website about:"Dr. Hidaia Alassouli Advertisements".

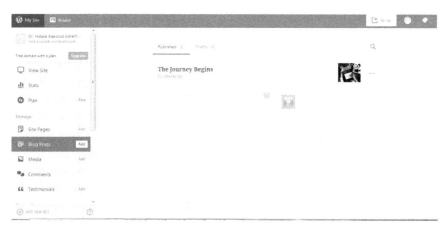

14) Creating word press website for advertisements in free webhosting www.000webhost.com:

1- As the wordpress.com web hosting can't give free web hosting with full capability so I can add plugins, I preferred to install word press from another free web hosting www.000webhost.com:

2- Go to the link https://www.000webhost.com/free-website-sign-up and signup

3- I named my website hidaia-adv.000webhost.com.

4- The control panel link https://www.000webhost.com/members/website/hidaia-adv/build

5- Choose install word press website to install the website directly. I put the username admin and the password admin. Your login page https://hidaia-adv.000webhostapp.com/wp-login.php.

6- You will get the following dashboard.

7- The dashboard link https://hidaia-adv.000webhostapp.com/wp-admin/

15) Creating advertisement links in Propeller Ads and using them in the blogger website:

1- This website is not profitable compared to Google AdSense as it gives you for 1000 views around 1 cent only while in goggle AdSense you can get for 1000 views 1 used.

2- Register in the advertising company Propeller Ads as publisher. Walk in the activation process and you will get the following picture. See the video https://www.youtube.com/watch?v=obiWL93NYog for explanation

3- Go to the advertisement website Propeller Ads to make advertisement. Add new site: halassouli-ad.blogspot.com. It will ask you to verify your website so it will be sure that it will be your website. It gave the following code to verify your web site:

<meta name="propeller" content="2f15184c91e91deddc305918efd6f6a7"/>

31

4- We go to web site halassouli-ad.blogspot.com again. Edit the theme. Paste the code under the head tag <head> and we paste the meta tag.

5- We click after that verify in the Propeller Ads site

6- : Create the zone. Choose between the following options.

7- Choose any one. Let's assume I chose Oneclick (Popunder) option and name the zone Popunder. We get the following code

<script type="text/javascript" src="//go.pub2srv.com/apu.php?zoneid=1612886"></script>

8- Paste it under the </html> tag in the blog theme html code.

9- To see other way to paste the advertisement in the blog. Create another zone. I made it popunder this time also. I got the following link:

```
<script type="text/javascript" src="//go.onclasrv.com/apu.php?zoneid=1614852"></script>
```

10- Go to your blogger in the link www.blogger.com. Go to layout. Then go to footer, any footer section. Press add gadget. Choose to insert html or java script. Insert the advertisement script

```
<script type="text/javascript" src="//go.onclasrv.com/apu.php?zoneid=1614852"></script>
```

11- To see smart direct ads. Create new zone and choose smart direct ads. I got the following link:

http://go.pub2srv.com/afu.php?zoneid=1614860

You can use the link anywhere to earn profits.

12- In the profile settings in Propeller Ads, you can enter payment information through PayPal account in the payment method section under

13- You can use hit leap or otohits or traffic spirit or any bot traffic tool discussed before to get traffic

16) Creating advertisement links in Propeller Ads and using them in the word press website:

1- You can see the video: https://www.youtube.com/watch?v=vcunFgelHDc

2- This website is not profitable compared to Google AdSense as it gives you for 1000 views around 1 cent only while in Google AdSense you can get for 1000 views 1 used.

3- Register in the advertising company Propeller Ads as publisher. Walk in the activation process and you will get the following picture.

4- Go to the advertisement website Propeller Ads to make advertisement. Add new site "hidaia-adv.000webhostapp.com". It will ask you to verify your website so it will be sure that it will be your website. It gave the following code to verify your web site:

<meta name="propeller" content="c47f487baeb6ad75d37a18c0f1977b1e">

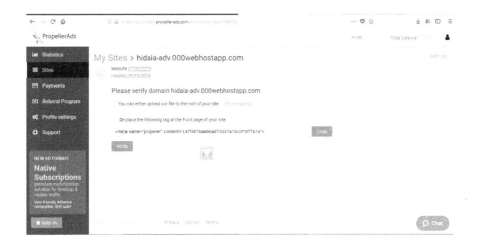

5- Click download the meta tag file. I had the name "c47f487baeb6ad75d37a18c0f1977b1e.html". Go to the main web hosting dashboard https://www.000webhost.com/members/website/hidaia-adv/build. Click file manager and upload the file.

6- In Propeller Ads, click verify to verify the website

7- Create new zone under the new web site. Let's name it "popunder". Choose the oneclick (popunder) advertisement option. And choose word press form. We get the zone id "1615110"

8- Go to your word press dashboard https://hidaia-adv.000webhostapp.com/wp-admin/. Go to appearance and then widgets. Choose the footer side one widget. Add new meta and insert on it the code: <meta name="propeller" content="c47f487baeb6ad75d37a18c0f1977b1e">

9- Go to your word press dashboard https://hidaia-adv.000webhostapp.com/wp-admin/. Go to plugin. Search for Propeller Ads plugin. Search for the Propeller Ads Official Plugin.

10- Install it and activate it. Otherwise, download and install and activate the plugin from internet. It can be found in https://wordpress.org/plugins/propellerads-official/

11- Go the Propeller Ads Official Plugin to configure it.

12- Check all buttons to be on and enter the zone id and anti-ad block token. You have to enable advertisement for logged on users to see the advertisement

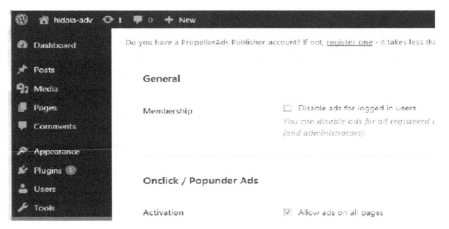

13- In the profile settings in Propeller Ads, you can enter payment information through PayPal account in the payment method section under.

14- Also you can test the referral. Go to referral section I got the referral in the banner section .My referral is:

<a   href="https://publishers.propellerads.com/#/pub/auth/signUp?refId=Tbw6"><img src="http://promo.propellerads.com/300x250_03.jpg" alt="Propeller Ads"></a>

15- .To use the referral in my website, go to the word press dashboard. Go to appearance and select widgets. Click the text option. I selected to add it in the footer 1.I put the title is "Earn money". I put on the box body the referral

<a href="https://publishers.propellerads.com/#/pub/auth/signUp?refId=Tbw6"><img src="http://promo.propellerads.com/300x250_03.jpg" alt="Propeller Ads" /></a>

16- The referral advertisement will appear in the footer of the website.

14- To see smart direct ads. Create new zone and choose smart direct ads. I got the following link:

http://go.oclaserver.com/afu.php?zoneid=1615825

You can use the link anywhere to earn profits.

15- You can use hit leap or otohits or traffic spirit or any bot traffic tool discussed before to get traffic

17) Creating advertisement links in revenuehits and using them in the blogger website:

1- See the video https://www.youtube.com/watch?v=obiWL93NYog for explanation.

2- Register in the advertisement website revenue hits https://www.revenuehits.com/. Fellow the registration steps. You will get the following after registration

3- Go to placements. Create new website : https://halassouli-ad.blogspot.com/

4- Choose new placement. I chose to be desktop advertisement. I chose to put the advertisement in the footer

5- Make a new footer placement. Get the code

```
<script                     data-cfasync='false'                     type='text/javascript'
src='//p276783.clksite.com/adServe/banners?tid=276783_535343_0&type=footer&size=37'></s
cript>
```

6- Go to to the blog. https://www.blogger.com. Go to theme. Go to Edit html. Before </html> tag, paste the advertisement code. Then make save. The code:

```
<script                     data-cfasync='false'                     type='text/javascript'
src='//p276783.clksite.com/adServe/banners?tid=276783_535343_0&type=footer&size=37'></s
cript>
```

7- It did not agree to save it and there was error. So we go and convert the code and paste it again. You can use the following web site to convert the code:

https://cnmu.blogspot.com/p/blog-page.html

8- The converted code:

<script   data-cfasync='false'   type='text/javascript' src='//p276783.clksite.com/adServe/banners?tid=276783_535343_0&type=f ooter&size=37'></script>

9- Copy the converted code and paste it again before the </html> tag in theme html code of the blog. Now you can see the advertisement in the footer of the blog: halassouli-ad.blogspot.com

10- - Getting money from Propeller Ads advertisement by direct link.

11- Otherwise you can paste the script other way. Make another placement. I chose to be sider advertisement. I got the code\

```
<script                data-cfasync='false'                type='text/javascript'
src='//p276783.clksite.com/adServe/banners?tid=276783_536062_0&type=slider&size=38'>
</script>
```

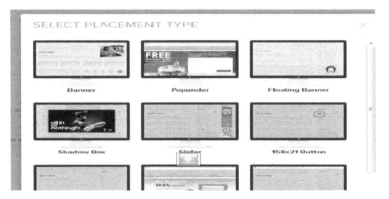

12- Go to the blogger www.blogger.com. Go to layout. Choose the sidebar-right-1. Write the script for the advertisement.

13- You can use hit leap or otohits or traffic spirit or any bot traffic tool discussed before to get traffic

18) Creating advertisement links in revenuehits and using them in the word press website:

1- See the video https://www.youtube.com/watch?v=obiWL93NYog for explanation.

2- Register in the advertisement website revenue hits https://www.revenuehits.com/. Fellow the registration steps. You will get the following after registration

3- Go to placements. Create new website : https://hidaia-adv.000webhostapp.com/

4- Choose new placement. I chose to be desktop advertisement. I chose to put the advertisement in the footer

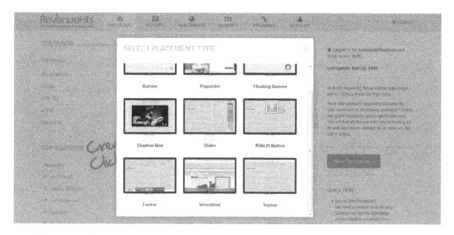

5- Make a new footer placement. Get the code

```
<script data-cfasync='false' type='text/javascript'
src='//p276783.clksite.com/adServe/banners?tid=276783_536074_0&type=footer&size=37'></scrip
t>
```

6- To use the advertisement in my website, go to the word press dashboard. Go to appearance and select widgets. Click the text option. I selected to add it in the footer 1. I put the title is "Adv". I put on the box body the advertisement script

```
<script data-cfasync='false' type='text/javascript'
src='//p276783.clksite.com/adServe/banners?tid=276783_536074_0&type=footer&size=37'></s
cript>
```

7- I tried to make pop under advertisement for the wordpress website halassouliadv.wordpress
   com. I paste it as text widget for test.

19) Earning money from advertisement links in CPAlead and using them in the word press website:

1. Register in the CPAlead website as publisher. You will get the following dashboard.

2. **-Super link:**

   - You can try to test super link option. When your visitor clicks on a Superlink on a social network or on your website, they will detect   visitor's device and country to display top CPA offer available to them. Works best with purchased pop under traffic.

   - I created a super link and I got the following

     <a href="https://viral782.com/index.html?b=66100&s=832026">Superlink</a>

   - I pasted it the word press site in new page named superlink. Its link is https://halassouliadv.wordpress.com/superlink/

3. **Custom Ad:**

   - You can try to test the custom ad. Choose the banner size (no of columns and no of rows), and iframe size . I named the banner to be custom ad 1.

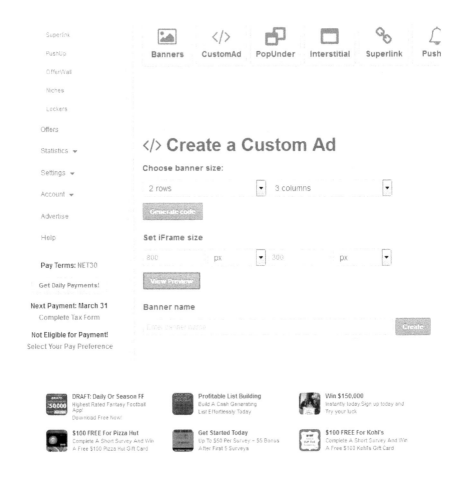

- Get the code. Place this code on your website in the area you would the banner ad to appear.

  <iframe   src='https://viral782.com/contact.html?id=66109' style='border:none;overflow:hidden;width: 800px; height: 300px'></iframe>

- Example, I pasted it the word press site in new page named customad. Its link, https://halassouliadv.wordpress.com/customad/

4. Popunder:

When your visitor clicks on a link that triggers a pop under ad on your website, the pop under ad will appear and you will earn money. You need to select how you want the pop under ad to open. Enter the following data

- Create popunder ad. You will get the below form. Fill the form. I named the name of css script to be popunder.css

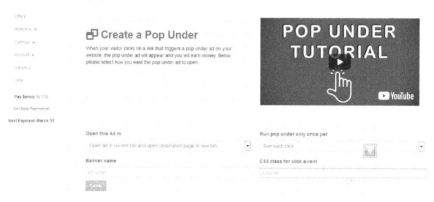

- You will get the following script Copy and paste this code anywhere on the website you want the ad to appear.Then remember the class you set when you created this ad. Assign this class to the link you want to trigger the ad. For example, if your class is "video_link" then any link that has video_link as a class will trigger the ad.

  <a href="http://www.google.com" class "popunder"> google </a>

  <script type="text/javascript" src="https://viral782.com/track.html?js=66128"></script>

- I pasted it the word press site in new page named popunder. Example: https://halassouliadv.wordpress.com/popunder. It did not work at all.

5. PushUp ad:

A PushUp ad will detect your visitor's device and country and ask them to interact with an advertisement in a notification prompt. When your visitor clicks OK, they will be sent to the ad and you will earn money. If they click cancel, the notification prompt will close. Fill the following details:

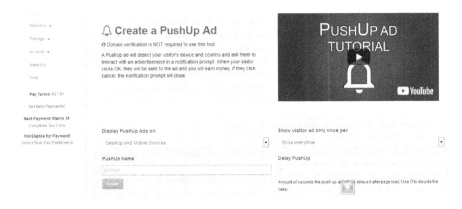

- Create the advertisement. Then get the code script. Place this code on the webpage you want the pushup ad to appear.

  <script type="text/javascript" src="https://viral782.com/track.html?js=66132"></script>

- I pasted it the word press site in new page named pushup. Example: https://halassouliadv.wordpress.com/pushup. But it did not work for me.

6. Banner:

- Go to banner option. Choose to create banner. Choose the banner size.

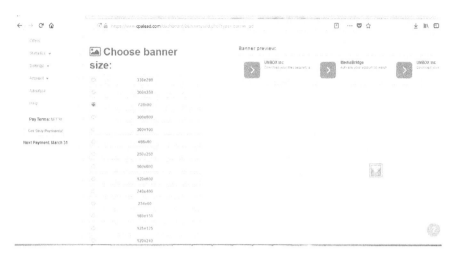

- Choose get banner code. That was my ad banner code

```
<script
src="https://viral782.com/track.html?pid=832026&id=66181&bid=4&w=300&h=600">
</script>
```

- Go to your website and paste the script code in the part you want the banner to be on it. Go to appearance, then widgets and then choose text. Choose the place to put the banner whether it is footer or sidebar. I chose sidebar. I created new widget in the side bar, and I pasted the code in text box.

7. **Interstitial Ad:**

- When your visitor clicks on a link that triggers an interstitial, they will be required to view a list of ads before they can access your webpage. If your visitor interacts with an ad, you will earn money. Enter the data in this form. I used the adjustable desktop theme. I named the class to be inters

- The output must be the following after clicking CPAlead link.

- I got the following code:

```
<script type="text/javascript" src="https://viral782.com/track.html?js=66313"></script>
```

- Copy and paste this code anywhere on the website you want the ad to appear. Then remember the class you set when you created this ad. Assign this class to the link you want to trigger the ad. For example, if your class is "video_link" then any link that has video_link as a class will trigger the ad.

```
<a href="http://www.google.com" class "inters"> google </a>
```

```
<script type="text/javascript" src="https://viral782.com/track.html?js=66313"></script>
```

- I pasted it the word press site in new page named inters. Example: https://halassouliadv.wordpress.com/inters/. Note: It did not work at all.

8. Sharing links and get payment payment per action:

You will get paid per action here, as example when signed up or made survey. But the advertisements restricted for the referral link to be opened in certain countries. You cant open it by proxy anywhere else in the world

- Here the images of offers

- For examples, lets take the offer "Get a $100 Amazon Gift Card!"

53

- I got the following link : "http://viral481.com/srv.html?id=3099540&pub=832026". It can open only in usa. But I tried to open it in free gate browser. It is the only browser it could open.

- When the customer completes the request, you will get the payment.

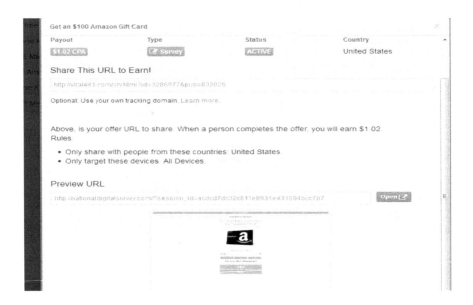

www.ingramcontent.com/pod-product-compliance
Lightning Source LLC
Chambersburg PA
CBHW071033050326
40689CB00014B/3629